The region gets no rainfall.

I arrived at 6:20 PM. Though it may have been closer to 6:30. It was still hot out and the air was incredibly dry. I recall the car thermometer reading 82 degrees, but it felt much warmer. The terrain was steep and barbed wire fences crisscrossed the hillsides. As I climbed a fence post I remembered the No Trespassing sign I saw earlier. Once over I started up immediately, at a fast pace. After 15 minutes or so I neared the cliff. You could smell the paint as if it was applied yesterday. I was surprised at how intact they were. I walked up close, thinking about this form of tradition. The sun reflected off the rocks hurting my eyes. Some of the marks were shinning, as if projecting light. The history of It all was overwhelming.

August 26 2014

ID
Colin Snapp
Études Books N°12
ISBN 978-2-36962-006-8

Photography by Colin Snapp
Edited and designed by Études Studio
Published by Études Books, Paris
www.etudes-studio.com
Image post production by Janvier
First edition, 500 copies
September 2015, printed in EU

1212

3
34
84

1234

20
48

1237

50
20
48

1240

1243

WES

1267

1270

1274

1281

28

1283

24

1297

1299

48

1305

1309

28

1321

49

35
42
49

35

1341

1353

34

23

1394

1401

1407